TO GRACE

... ARE'NT YOU LUCKY THAT
YOU HAVE SUCH WONDERFUL
PARENTS!

Steve Curtis

04/26/2018

The Brier Patch

Published by The Brier Patch, LLC
Evans, GA.
ISBN # 978-0-9964374-2-4
Visit us on the web at www.thebrierpatch.com.

`Publisher's Cataloging-in-Publication Data
provided by Five Rainbows Cataloging Services

Names: Beech, Deanna. | Lester, Steven P., illustrator.
Title: But aren't I lucky that… / Deanna Beech ; [illustrated by] Steven P. Lester.
Description: Evans, GA : The Brier Patch, 2016. | Summary: Tiger is excited about the big game, like anyone would be,
but when things don't go his way, can he still find what makes him lucky?

Identifiers: ISBN 978-0-9964374-0-0 (pbk.) | ISBN 978-0-9964374-2-4 (hardcover) | ISBN 978-0-9964374-1-7 (EPUB)
Subjects: CYAC: Winning and losing--Fiction. | Optimism--Fiction. | Resilience (Personality trait)--Fiction. | Conduct of life--Fiction. | BISAC: JUVENILE
FICTION / Social Themes / Self-Esteem & Self-Reliance. | JUVENILE FICTION / General. | JUVENILE FICTION / Health & Daily Living / General.
Classification: LCC PZ7.1.B443 Bu 2016 (print) | LCC PZ7.1.B443 (ebook) | DDC [Fic]--dc23.

But Aren't I Lucky That...

By Deanna Beech

Illustrated by Steven Lester

For my amazing children, Foster and Bryce, who share their special moments with me every day.

Deanna Beech

For Rosemary, Russ and Anna. They are my heart's delight.

Steven Lester

"Time to get up!" Mom called from the kitchen.

I pulled the pillow tightly over my ears. I was having the best dream ever…
"Bases are loaded. The batter's up. The pitch… YES! It's going… going… a home run!"

"Breakfast's ready! Come on now, Tiger. Get up."

I did. Slowly.

My eyes were still shut as the cheering of the crowd gave way to passing cars and birds chirping. And, of course, there were the sounds from my neighbors, like the news station Mr. Jones always has on in the morning.

I took a deep breath and stretched.

"What's that? Bacon! Oh boy, I love that smell."

Mom likes to make what she calls "real food" on Saturdays. So instead of cereal, which doesn't really have a smell, we get eggs with toast and bacon. It smelled so good, and I was so comfy, that I laid back and thought, "Aren't I lucky? Today's a great day!"

"Bye, Tiger!" Dad called. I jumped out of bed and ran to the kitchen so I could get a good bye hug.

Just as I got to the table, it happened.

Daddy bent over to kiss Maya. At the same time, Maya reached up for Daddy, and her hands were covered in jelly. Daddy didn't see it. He was talking to Mom. And she got him right in the middle of his shirt.

Daddy let out a loud, "UGH!"

I froze. Yuck. What a mess!

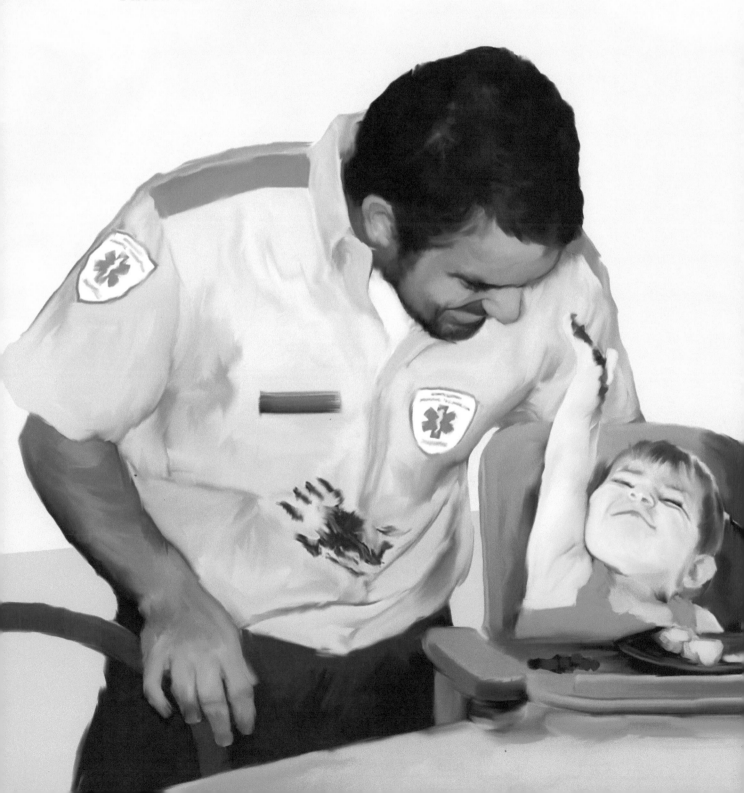

But Daddy laughed. "I've been jellied. Maya the jelly monster got me. But aren't I lucky, I have more clean shirts?"

"Wow," I thought, "that is lucky."

"I'll be back by dinner," he said as I got my bear hug. "Good luck at the game, Tiger! Can't wait to hear all about it at dinner." He ruffled my hair and headed out the door.

I stared down at my plate.

"What's wrong?" Mom asked.

"I wish Daddy could come to my game." I poked at my toast.

"You know he'd be there if he could."

I sighed.

"And, you're right," Mom said. "It is a bummer. But remember, there's always more than one way to look at it."

"What do you mean?" I asked.

"Well, aren't we lucky Daddy has a good job?" Mom asked.

"Yeah, I guess."

"And aren't all the people Daddy helps lucky because he's good at his job?

"Yeah. That's good."

"And aren't we lucky that his job, and mine, lets us buy yummy bacon and eggs? And—"

"And jelly toast."

Mom laughed. "Yes, and jelly toast."

"I get it. That is lucky," I said as I made my super favorite—
a bacon, egg, and jelly toast sandwich.

Yummmmmm…

Mom said we had to head out early because she had errands to do before the game. As we were walking out, we saw Ms. Wong coming home. She was carrying a bag of groceries so full all I could see was her feet.

"Mom, do you think she can see where she's going?" A second later, I got my answer. Ms. Wong tripped and fell on the sidewalk.

"Ohhhh!" She cried.

"Ms. Wong!" Mom rushed over. "Are you okay?"

"Oh, my ankle hurts," Ms. Wong said, touching it carefully.

"You came down on it pretty hard," said Mom. "Here, let's help you up, and we'll put some ice on it."

It took some time to get Ms. Wong settled and her groceries put away. I was getting worried that we'd be late for the game.

"There you go." Mom handed her some hot tea. "Feeling better?"

Ms. Wong leaned back in her chair. "Yes. Much better."

"Good. Now try to stay off it as much as you can. We'll stop by tomorrow to see how you're doing."

"Boy, it was lucky we were there to help Ms. Wong," I said.

"Yes." Mom smiled at me. "Tell me—how do you feel right now?"

"Really good."

Mom buckled her seatbelt and leaned over to whisper, "That's one of life's little secrets."

"What secret?"

"When you do something for someone else, they feel good, but you feel even better."

You know what? It did feel good.

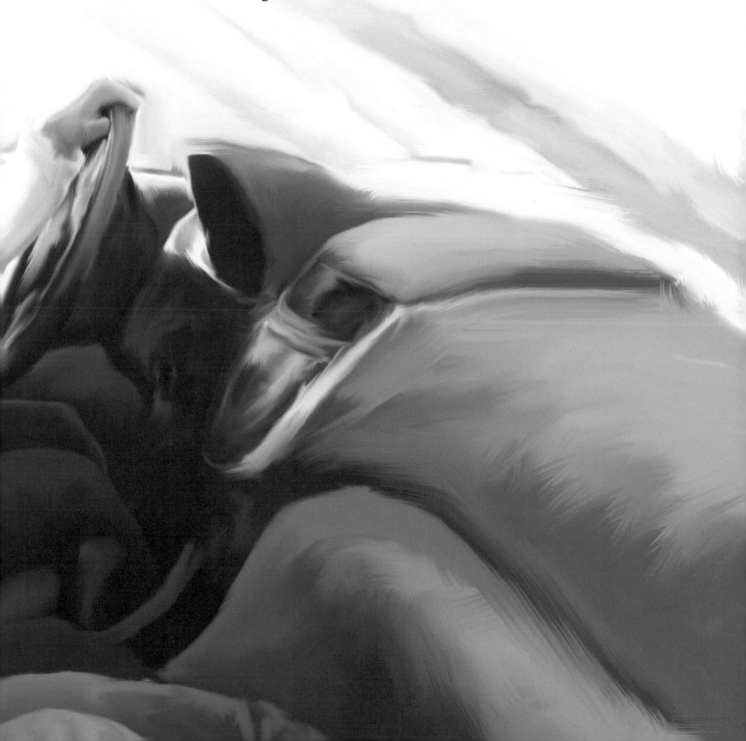

We skipped the errands so we wouldn't be late. I was glad, too, because I got to practice with Derik and Jada. Jada's our best batter. I was running after one of her ground balls when Coach called us over.

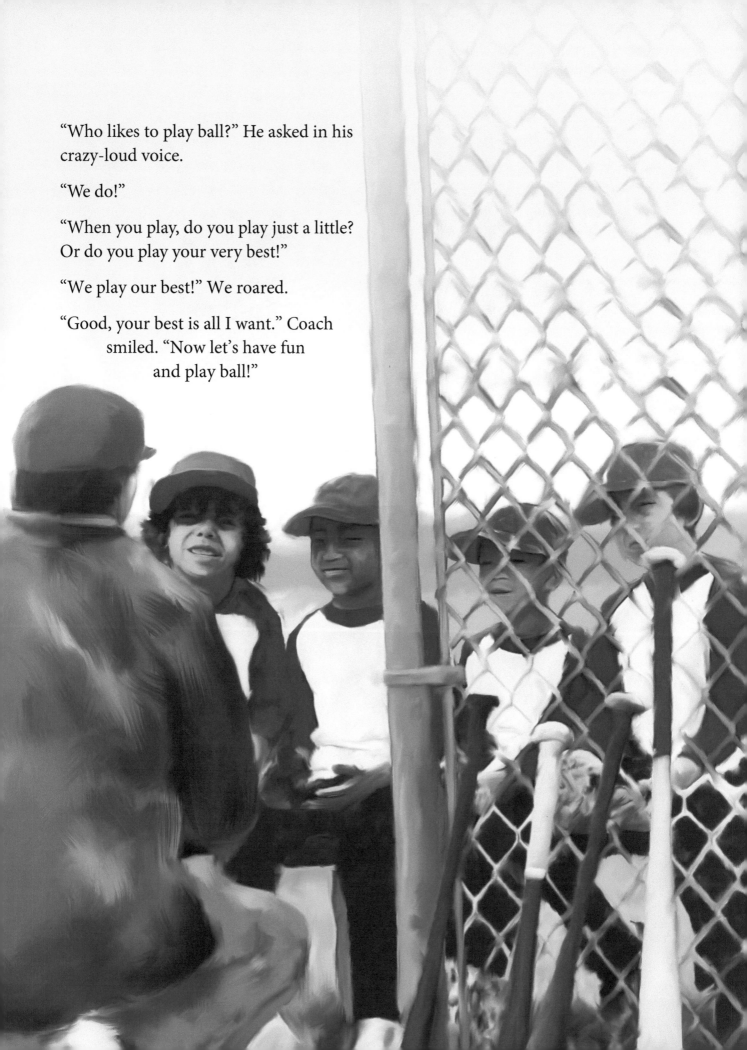

"Who likes to play ball?" He asked in his crazy-loud voice.

"We do!"

"When you play, do you play just a little? Or do you play your very best!"

"We play our best!" We roared.

"Good, your best is all I want." Coach smiled. "Now let's have fun and play ball!"

Right off the bat, I knew we were in trouble. Fly balls kept soaring over my head. They sailed past me, hit the ground with a bounce, and kept rolling. I lost count of how many. The scoreboard didn't. They were crushing us. I was upset and out of breath from all the running around.

"OK, focus," I told myself. "Keep your eye on the ball and breathe slowly. You can do this." That's what Coach says to do. So I did it.

Right then, Billy Howard came up to bat. Billy is their best batter. They call him "The Hammer." He was pretty scary, but I was ready.

The pitcher threw the ball. Billy swung. Crack! It went way high heading right to me. I kept my eye on it as I ran backwards. I lined up my glove with the ball and…

SMACK! I caught it! Can you believe it? I caught Billy Howard's fly ball.

The crowd started hollering and whistling and clapping.

"Way to go, Tiger!" Mom yelled.

Even Coach was jumping up and down. And the super best part? Billy Howard was out. I felt like a million bucks!

I wished the game could have ended right then, but it didn't. Like I said, they were crushing us. We kept chasing their balls around, and they kept getting their runners in. We lost big time, and it felt terrible.

Coach sat us all down.

"You gave it your best," he said. "We'll learn from this one." But it didn't help.

I was quiet on the way to the car. Mom knew why.

"You're upset you lost the game, aren't you?"

I didn't answer.

"I know it's tough to lose," she said, "especially when you tried so hard. But aren't you lucky you had a chance to play with your friends?"

"Yeah, that part was fun," I sighed.

"And… now you tell me one," she urged. "Go ahead. What else was lucky?"

"Well…" I remembered the sting of Hammer's ball and rubbed my hand. "I did catch that fly ball. That was pretty okay."

"Pretty okay?" She teased. "Are you kidding? That ball was going super-fast. That was an amazing catch. Did you hear me screaming? I was so excited."

"Yeah, I could hear you. I think everyone in the park could hear you."

We were laughing now, and that's when it hit me. Sure, we lost the game. That part was a bummer. But it wasn't all bad. There were some pretty good parts, too.

I told Mom what I was thinking.

"I love those brains," she said. "How'd you get so smart?"

That night, while we were setting the table for dinner, Daddy came home.
Maya and I ran to him like we always do. He swooped her up and gave me a
big one-armed hug.

"How did the game go, Tiger?"

I shrugged. "We lost."

Daddy put a hand on my shoulder. "I'm sorry."

"It's okay. It wasn't all bad. I made a really great catch. Didn't I Mom? I caught Billy Howard's fly ball. He's The Hammer, and he hit the ball really hard, but I caught it. And he was out."

"Wow, that is something," Daddy laughed.

"And before that, we helped Ms. Wong when she fell."

"Oh no, is she okay?" Daddy glanced over at Mom, who smiled and nodded.

"She is now. Mom and I took care of her. And that's when Mom told me about the secret."

"What secret?"

"You know, how when you help someone, they feel good but you feel even better. And you know what that means?"

"No, what does that mean?"

"It means you're the luckiest guy in the world because you get to help people every day."

Daddy grinned. "You're absolutely right. I'm the luckiest guy in the world, and you're one smart kid!"

Yeah, I knew that…
            and super lucky, too!

Authors Notes

A note to the grown ups

Your choice to read this book to your child shows that you are already doing the second most important thing that a parent can do – Begin with the end in mind. The first most important thing is obvious – Love the ba-geez-zes out of them.

The problem is that the 'second most important thing' is also the hardest thing in childrearing. If we want our kids to grow to be happy and successful adults, then we have to figure backward from there and inform our choices about what is important today. In short, we are all trying to figure out – What can we do now to teach our children how to be happy and successful in the future?

This is where it gets complicated. A moments worth of trying to define what happy and successful mean gets pretty convoluted. After we throw out the commercialized idea that happy equals spending money on entertainment (food, drinks, toys, movies, etc…) and successful equals having expensive things (cars, jewelry, electronics, etc…) we get closer to the heart of the matter –What makes people genuinely happy and successful in life?

Thankfully, we no longer have to guess. Research shows that a lot of what makes people happy and successful has to do with their style of thinking. Pessimistic thinking tends to lead to a negative view of situations and results in a less happy lifestyle, while optimistic thinking leads to a positive view of situations and a happier, even healthier, lifestyle.

We all have a style of thinking – a set of assumptions based on experience. It is our default setting for the skills that we bring to new situations. And if it is skills that we're talking about … then it can be taught. To this end, we took the important concepts that have been shown to correlate with genuine happiness in life and developed a story that teaches them to children. For a more information on the concepts and skills covered in this book, along with additional resources, please join us at http://www.thebrierpatch.com/Parent-Resources.html.

And remember… there is no such thing as a perfect parent; but, by loving them, learning with them, and striving for our best we will be good enough.

Deanna Beech

Illustrators Notes

A universal language

What a joy it has been to work on this delightful project! As a seasoned artist, I have discovered how rewarding it is to use those gifts I have been blessed with for positive influence and human good.

As a parent of two foreign born children who have each experienced their share of disappointments and distressing events, I was thrilled to connect with Dr. Beech and immediately resonated with her work helping others to redirect thoughts and minimize stress.

I also was delighted to join her in creating a book designed to transfer those skills to parents and children. It's one thing to understand and appreciate those concepts. It's another thing altogether to make it simple enough that a child can comprehend and emulate.

We set out to illustrate a characters that any child could relate to, regardless of gender, race or social status. The models I used for the paintings were very diverse. They were not only from the United States, but also from Brazil, Trinidad and Puerto Rico.

The message of this story is universal to anyone, and we hope will reinforce excellent and resilient attitudes. As an artist and illustrator, my hope is than any child, regardless of his or her circumstances, can personalize the lessons in this story.

Steven Lester

Resiliency Tools

We all want to provide our children with a safe, happy and healthy development. And still, our children will have to cope with stress and face disappointments. Most of these are little obstacles, like having a fight with a friend or not doing well on a test. But, others are more intense, like moving to a new neighborhood or dealing with a divorce.

Not only is it inevitable that children will experience stress, it is an essential part of their self-development. They learn from these struggles and, as a result, they develop a set of tools. These are the ready-to-turn-to ways that they cope with and respond to difficulties. For example, some situations require a hammer, like when you to stand up for yourself in a strong aggressive way. While other situations require some polish, like when you mend a misunderstanding with someone. These tools form their personal toolbox. If we then intentionally help our children develop healthy tools it becomes a resiliency toolbox.

The Tools covered in 'But Aren't I Lucky That…'

Cognitive Reframing
The book's title is an easy to remember way to reframe negative thoughts. It's so catchy that kids readily pick it up and start to use it. By saying the word "BUT" after a negative thought, you negate it. It discredits what came before. It opens the possibility to have an alternative thought. If that thought is prompted to be positive by the statement "AREN'T I LUCKY THAT…" a more balanced view of the situation can emerge. It doesn't change what's real, but it does make it easier to accept the difficult situations. In the book, Tiger's mom illustrates this process when she helps Tiger think through the disappointment that Daddy can't come to the big game. She does it again when Tiger's team loses the game.

Acts of Kindness
This is the "secret" that Tiger's mom shares. She explains the truth that when we do something kind for someone else we actually are the ones that benefit the most. The person that we have been kind to gets to feel good, but we feel even better. Take a moment and recall the feeling you get when you hold the door for someone whose hands are full. It feels good. Something super small like that, it feels good. Now imagine if we (all of us) were to give more 'random acts of kindness.' Not only would we feel better, the world around us would be better.

Grit

Grit is the ability to be resilient in the face of failure and adversity. It's the 'get up' and 'keep going' when things get difficult, a key factor in success. This is obviously the hard part. When we are good at something and it comes easily to us, it feels good and is fun to do. We naturally want do more of it. But, things don't stay easy if you're really going to improve. For example, Tiger is good at baseball and loves playing it, but to become better he will have to keep trying even when he plays against other kids that are bigger and better. By sticking to it, he is showing grit.

Mindfulness

The concept of mindfulness is on the very first page. It is portrayed as Tiger wakes up and takes a moment to notice the sounds, smells and feeling of his room. In this way he is being mindful. Mindfulness is the act of being present in the moment. Experiencing what you see, what you smell, what you hear, what you taste, what you touch and what is touching you. By being more present in the moment, we become calm and more focused. It sounds simple, and it is. It is also powerful. Recent studies have found that using mindfulness exercises has verifiable benefits for those that are experiencing severe stress and anxiety such as Panic Disorder and Post Traumatic Stress Disorder.

Empathic Listening and Emotional Validation

At several times in the story, Tiger's mom shows empathic listening (when Tiger's Dad has to go to work and can't go to the game, and when Tiger's team loses the game). Empathic listening is really listening and letting the other person know that you can relate to how they feel. It's an important skill for children to learn. They learn it from us. When we take the time to listen and show that we understand, they learn to do the same. By modeling the behavior that we want our kids to emulate, we are teaching them. And better yet, we are relating to them.

To learn more about how to help your children develop these, and other, resiliency tools please visit the Resiliency Tool Box at www.thebrierpatch.com.

CPSIA information can be obtained
at www.ICGtesting.com
Printed in the USA
LVHW07n0603280618
582167LV00022B/197/P